T0145049

God Is with You
Wherever You Go

"Have I not commanded you? Be strong and courageous. Do not be afraid; do not be discouraged, for the LORD your God will be with you wherever you go."

—Joshua 1:9

This Book Belongs To:

_____

"For he will command His angels concerning you, to guard you in all your ways."

—Psalm 91:11

God Is with You Wherever You Go

Jessica Kesler

Copyright © 2023 Jessica Kesler.

All rights reserved. No part of this book may be used or reproduced by any means,
graphic, electronic, or mechanical, including photocopying, recording, taping or by any
information storage retrieval system without the written permission of the author
except in the case of brief quotations embodied in critical articles and reviews.

This book is a work of non-fiction. Unless otherwise noted, the author and the publisher
make no explicit guarantees as to the accuracy of the information contained in this book and
in some cases, names of people and places have been altered to protect their privacy.

WestBow Press books may be ordered through booksellers or by contacting:

WestBow Press
A Division of Thomas Nelson & Zondervan
1663 Liberty Drive
Bloomington, IN 47403
www.westbowpress.com
844-714-3454

Because of the dynamic nature of the Internet, any web addresses or links contained in this
book may have changed since publication and may no longer be valid. The views expressed
in this work are solely those of the author and do not necessarily reflect the views of
the publisher, and the publisher hereby disclaims any responsibility for them.

Any people depicted in stock imagery provided by Getty Images are models,
and such images are being used for illustrative purposes only.
Certain stock imagery © Getty Images.

ISBN: 979-8-3850-0676-2 (sc)
ISBN: 979-8-3850-0677-9 (hc)
ISBN: 979-8-3850-0678-6 (e)

Library of Congress Control Number: 2023917182

Print information available on the last page.

WestBow Press rev. date: 11/17/2023

WestBow
PRESS®
A DIVISION OF THOMAS NELSON
& ZONDERVAN

This book is made for God, our Lord and Savior Jesus Christ, and dedicated to all his children of the world. May you always know you're made with great purpose, are highly loved, and wonderful. Reach for the stars!

To Ari, Ella and Asher—
my beautiful family and greatest blessing,
I love you! This is always for you.

In your mother's womb,
God formed you with
His own two hands.
He set you apart and created
you to achieve great plans!

From the moment you
were born and took your
very first breath of air,
God promised to be with you
so you would always know
He is a Father who loves
you and will always care.

God sends an angel to guard
you in all your ways,
From morning to night all
while you dance, sing, and play!

He's written His Word
to teach and provide you
unconditional wisdom,
All while He protects
and watches you from
His great kingdom.

God is most powerful
and is there to help you
whenever you may need.
So don't ever fear, my dear;
Be strong and courageous—
He can turn any situation
around so you may succeed!

God gives us free will so we can think and act on our own And has blessed us with a voice inside called the Holy Spirit to help guide us along.

That voice inside tells us
what is OK and not so good.
So listen closely, my dear: He
tells us all things we shouldn't
do and really should.

And when we listen and
follow His instruction,
Our path is set straight—
free from obstruction.

So when we do face
challenges, big or small,
God wants us not to
worry and just trust Him.
He will not let us fall!

God guards and protects us. He holds us in His hands so tight. He is stronger than anything and loves you with all His might!

God is with us in every
stage as we grow.
Through every moment
in life, His love is like the
rivers that endlessly flow.

Through happy times and sad,
From birth to old age,
You can always count on God.
He never leaves us;
He never fades.

You are His great masterpiece
and one very special child to God.
So, surely, you should
always know that God is
with you wherever you go!

Printed in the United States
by Baker & Taylor Publisher Services